iPhone Book
For Seniors

Explore the features of the iPhone XS and iPhone XS
Max with ease; including tips for maintaining and
troubleshooting your iPhone

Stephen K. Stone

Dedicated to all my readers

Table of Contents

Acknowledgement

I want to say a very big thank you to Miriam Stone, my daughter. She gave me moral support throughout the process of writing this book.

Acknowledgement

I want to say a very big thank you to Miriam Stone, my daughter. She gave me moral support throughout the process of writing this book.

INTRODUCTION

Thanks for getting a copy of this book. Once a year, in the fall, all old iPhones turn into rotten apples. Owners are tormented by doubts: whether to update? Couch analysts vehemently criticize Apple for its lack of ideology, Apple shares fall briefly, and a few minutes after the presentation releases a review of the new iPhone X. Comic, albeit truthful. And when the dust settles a little, it is time to review. Apple officially presented its new phones, called XS, XS Max and XR. The company made sure to offer several improvements, mainly related to the equipment. Models use a 7 nm A12 processor. It is faster than its predecessor and consumes less energy. This book, however, concerns itself with only the iPhone XS and XS Max

You will find the following information:
- Overview of your smartphone
- Description of Design and Display
- Information about The software of your iPhone
- Information about iOS 12
- Troubleshooting
- Tips & Tricks for your iPhone

It's time to learn something new about your iPhone. Now start savoring the contents of this user guide.

Differences between iPhone XS and iPhone XS Max

iPhone XS

Apple announced the introduction of the iPhone XS on September 12 2018. And it features one of the most advanced tech hat you can find in an Apple phone. The iPhone XS takes on the look of the iPhone X and you would hardly tell the difference.

It is 5.8 inch in size and the screen features an OLED display that is said to be one of the sharpest. The density of the pixels to is top notch supporting wide color, Dolby vision, HDR 10 and others. The glass in the smartphone is exceptionally durable and the resistance too has been improved.

Just as you would find in the iPhone X, the iPhone XS has a stainless steel frame and glass on the body that makes it able to be wirelessly charged. It also comes along with a TrueDepth camera that is just awesome for Face ID. The Face ID system debuted in the iPhone X and it has been in iPhones catalogue ever since.

You can get the option to choose from the option for color gold, which is a new option for iPhones. And just like its predecessors, iPhone XS is equipped with water and dust resistance. But it's not like the older iPhones. It's been upgraded to IP68. With the new improvement, you are protected against splashes or spills of liquid.

This is an improvement from the iPhone X IP67 rating. With the IP68 of the iPhone XS, that just means the ability of withstand water can hold as deep as 6.6 feet or 2 meters. And this can last as long as 30 minutes. When they say IP68, the number 6 stands for the ability to resist dust and the number 8 stand for the ability to resist water.

With the high number of water resistance and dust, you can say that you are protected fully from dirt and dust. The device will very well survive splashes, or drops of rain. If it is exposed in water accidentally, you don't have to worry about the phone having fault.

In the iPhone XS, you'll find a 7 nanometer bionic chip. With the 4 core GPU that you find in the A12, performance has been increased by 50% over the former A11 chip of the iPhone X

The 2 high performance cores that you find in the iPhone XS A12 are faster that the iPhone X A11 chip by 15%. So with the bigger battery of the iPhone XS and the introduction of the A 12 bionic, you will have longer battery life for the device. it's is said that the battery of the iPhone XS lasts about 30 minutes longer than the iPhone X. and it's a relief to see Apple stepping up their game in battery life.

The storage too is able to hold up to 512 GB. But you can opt for the other kind of storage space like the 256GB or the 64GB. There also an 8 core natural engine that is said to be able to complete about 5 trillion operations for each second. This will really benefit apps and games that makes use of the AR feature.

For the iPhone XS, you still get the 12 megapixel dual camera that was in the iPhone X. but the fact that the megapixels are the same does not mean that the camera capabilities are the same. Of course with great power comes great camera. There have been some major upgrades to the iPhone XS camera.

With the wide-angle sensor bigger now, you'll be able to get your pictures sharper not only in daylight, but also in low light. It's is also equipped with smart HDR and this helps to get some more detail in the photos and just make it look better. It brings out the colors more and balances out the shadows and the highlight.

It has a 2x optical zoom telephoto lens that makes it possible to use portrait mode. With this you get more blurring to the background and a classier bokeh. Plus there's a new feature that they call the depth control. What this does is that it makes you able to adjust the depth of field for the photo you want to capture.

The true tone flash also got an improvement in the iPhone XS. There's a 32 percent larger sensor that makes videos better when you are capturing in low light.

The TrueDepth camera still uses the 7 megapixels lends that you can use for Face ID. You can also make use of this for image that you want to take with the camera facing front. The TrueDepth camera also got an upgrade so that the processing of the Face ID can be faster. Which only means that you don't have to waste time for the camera recognizes your face and continues with authentication.

The rear camera of the iPhone XS has a 2 lens camera setup just like the iPhone X. This comes with a 12 megapixel f/1.8 wide angles lens with a focal length of 26mm.

coupled with another 12 megapixel f/2.4 telephoto lens with a focal length of 56m. This makes 2x optical zoom available. And when you combine both digital zoon and optical zoom, you can get up to 10 x zoom. With the 2 lenses of the iPhone XS, you get optical image stabilization and features wide angle support. There's also been improvement in the photo quality of the rear camera which makes the XS better than the X.

The other features in the iPhone XS include, the Gigaitcas LTE support, Bluetooth 5.0 along with dual SIM option. You can make use of 2 phone numbers at once with the option to use both eSIM and nano-SIM. Unlike the iPhone X, the iPhone is equipped with more LTE bands.

For the normal 64GB storage of the iPhone XS, it is priced at $999. But that's not the only option for the prices and storage. For the higher storage of 256GB it's priced at $1,149 and for the 512GB it's $1,349

iPhone XS Max

The iPhone X launched a new design for the line of iPhone and the iPhone XS Max showed us that Apple has no arrangement to change the design. It still took the same format and design except for one very obviously thing

The iPhone XS Max is big. Yes it truly is 'Max'. While the iPhone XS is no small phone, the iPhone XS Max is incredibly huge with a screen of 6.5 inches. While a big screen sounds exciting for cool HD movies and fantastic high resolution games, it might not be for everybody.

It still has the same stainless steel and glass design as the iPhone X and iPhone XS. It features an edge to edge display and it supports wireless charging that is said to be a bit faster as well as Face ID. The TrueDepth camera of the iPhone makes the Face ID recognition possible. This option too has gotten faster but it still won't work when switched to landscape orientation

The iPhone XS Max is the biggest of the X trio. But the size doesn't affect its weight that much. What surprises most people about the iPhone XS Max is the way it feel light despite its massive screen. Of course it is heavier that the iPhone 8 plus but not as much, and you might not even notice.

If you've been used to carrying any iPhone that's on the plus side of things, then you shouldn't have much problem handling the iPhone XS Max. But if you are used to the small 4.7 – 5 inch iPhones, then you might want to get pants with bigger pockets because the XS Max won't fit as much.

When you take a look at the top right corner of the iPhone XS Max, you'll find something like a band. There are the 2 antenna lines and you'll find that cuts right in the upper right of the stainless steel and the other one wrapped in the bottom left of the device. And you'll also easily notice that the bottom speaker holes are not symmetrical again.

Another thing that the iPhone XS Max is equipped with is the option for dual-SIM support. For some countries it is not popular to see phones that feature dual-SIM. And there are many who would like to manage double numbers at once or more than one data plan at the same time with the same phone with buying another device.

You can just easily fix the SIM card the normal way through the SIM card tray. But this tray can only accommodate just one nano SIM card. But if you would like to activate another SIM, you can just make use of an eSIM. All this means is that you have a SIM but its jus the digital version of it.

All you just need to get your eSIM working is just scanning a QR code then going through with the given prompts. In some countries where the feature for dual SIM is very common and people can just change network carriers, you'll find the iPhone XS Max with double slots for nano SIM

Then you also have the new improved IP rating of the iPhone XS Max that has improved water resistance. The water resistance was in iPhone 7 and iPhone 8 but it features IP67 water and dust resistance. Even the iPhone X still comes with IP67.

What this means is that be submerged for just 3 feet for 30 minutes.

But with the iPhone XS Max, you have the rating at IP68. And this doubles the rating of the previous iPhones as it can last being in water as deep as 6 feet for 30 minutes. This improvement is not very visible just I sure will come in handy when you're at a pool party.

The iPhone XS Max is available in silver and space grey. The gold color only just came to wrap things up. While the gold effect has been on iPhone since iPhone 5, the iPhone XS Max just has this polishing of the stainless steel with the gold underneath. You also get this metallic look to the iPhone XS mac back.

The iPhone XS Max features an OLED display that will get your blacks darker, a more wider and vibrant dynamic range, increased power efficiency and higher brightness. The iPhone XS Max also has super retina display that features HDR support

The 6.5 inch iPhone XS Max features a 2,688 x 1,242 resolution for the screen. And this is a nice improvement from the iPhone XS that is only 5.8 and gives about 2,436 x 1,123 resolution. The screen of the iPhone XS Max still remains at 458 PIP (pixels per inch) so you know that you are getting your screen really sharp.

The iPhone XS Max is powered by the A12 bionic chip which is really no different from the iPhone XS. It has a 64 bit chip that features 6 cores and the 2 performance cores that is able to give a faster CPU power of up to 15 percent. The rest of the 4 are what they call high efficiency cores that makes use of less power about 50 percent compared to the A11.

The iPhone XS Max rear camera is not as different from the iPhone XS. But it does feature a 12 megapixel camera. And it has one of the cameras with a wide angle les with aperture of f/1.8 and then other of at 2x telephoto lens and aperture of f/2.4. It has an optical image stabilization that helps to decrease the amount of shakiness to an image.

For video, you still get the same 4K resolution at up to 60 fps for a normal recording. You can also shoot at 240 fps at 1080p if you would like to take your video slow-mo

II

Setting up your iPhone XS and iPhone XS Max

It doesn't matter if you coming new into the Apple family or you want to ditch your old iPhone, you will want to set up your iPhone before you start using it. And we are going to talk about how you can set up your iPhone XS and iPhone XS Max from the get go to the last step.

There are many ways that you can choose to setup your iPhone. You can either choose to start new, get some content from a different iPhone or transfer from a phone that's not an Apple product.

- **Setting up as new**. What this means is that you'll have to start fresh. Every feature and setting will be from scratch. If you have not used a smartphone or you just want to get that brand new feeling for your iPhone.
- **Restore data from iPad, iPhone or iPod**. You'll have to go online for this and navigate the iCloud. You can also transfer through iTunes. If you have use an iOS device previously, then this option is for you
- **Import for a non-Apple device**. If you have an android phone, windows phone or blackberry, you can still make the data transfer. You can use some online service to help you make the switch

When you turn your iPhone on for the first time, you'll see the Hello page show up in different language options. It doesn't matter if you are switching from an iPhone, restoring from android or stating as new, you'll see this screen.

1. Choose the **Slide to set up** then you want to swipe your finger through the screen for you to begin
2. Choose the language of your choice
3. Choose your preferred country
4. Choose a Wi-Fi network. But if a Wi-Fi network is not available at the moment of setting up, you can still register is later. For now choose **Cellular** instead.
   - You can decide to select the option for **Automatic Setup** at the stage. This is will set your iPhone with the same passwords, and settings at the previous iPhone. But if you selected the option set up the iPhone manually, you can just go through with the next step

5. When you read the data & privacy info about Apple, you can then choose **Continue**
6. Select **Enable Location Services**. If you would not like to enable location services now, you just choose **Skip Location Service**. But you can still enable it later on manually
7. Now you want to set up Face ID.
8. Set your passcode. You can set up a normal passcode of 6 digits, or you can just make a 4 digit passcode.
9. You will now be asked if you would like to set up your iPhone as new, transfer from a backup or restore from an android device

Setting up as new

If this is your first time using an iPhone, or you just don't want to your old data from to your previous smartphone to be transferred to the iPhone XS, then you can just start over on a clean slate. All you have to do is

1. Choose the option for **Set up as new iPhone**
2. Input your own Apple ID and password. If you have not created one, you can just choose the **Don't have an Apple ID**? Option to create
3. **Agree** to the terms and conditions
4. Select **Agree** to re-confirm
5. You want to set up **Apple Pay**
6. You want to set up **iCloud Keychain**
7. Set up the **Siri** feature and also the option for **Hey Siri**
8. If you want to set diagnostic information to Apple when the applications crashes. You can choose the **Send Diagnostic Information to Apple** option. If you don't want to send, choose **Don't send**
9. If you want, you can enable **Display zoom**
10. Select the option to **Get started**

Transfer from old iPhone to iPhone XS and XS Max

Using automatic setup for the iPhone

1. Choose your language in your new iPhone XS and keep your devices close together

2. When the pop up to set up your new iPhone with Apple ID comes up, select **Continue** to proceed.

3. Now you want to scan the image of that shows up in your new iPhone with your old iPhone.

4. Input the passcode that you used for your old iPhone on your new iPhone

5. Set up the option for **Face ID** in your new iPhone

6. Now you want to choose between the option of restoring the most recent backup available on your new iPhone or not to. Since we want to restore, you will select that option

7. Chose the option to restore from iCloud or iTunes
8. Read the terms and conditions and agree to it.
9. Select **Continue** under the option for **Express settings**. This will use the setting for location, sir and other options that were transferred from the old iPhone to the new iPhone.

Transfer from android device

1. When you set up your iPhone and you get to the **Apps and data** screen, select the option for **Move data from android**
2. Open up the **Google Play Store** in your android device and then look for **Move to iOS**
3. When the app shows up, select it
4. Choose **Install** to install it on your android device

5. Accept the request for permissions
6. Open up the app when it's been installed
7. Select the option for **Continue** on the two devices
8. On your android device, choose the **Agree** then **Next** option.
9. Enter in your android device the 12 digit code that is shown on your new iPhone device

When you enter in the code, the android device will be connected to the iPhone XS through peer to peer connection and you can choose which data you want to transfer. If you want to, you can also transfer from your Google account info for easy access to apps like chrome or other media.

The data that you selected will be transferred from your android device to your new iPhone and it will be placed it in the right sections that it should be in. The devices will be disconnected and android will ask you to take the phone to an Apple store for recycling

When you have transferred the necessary data, you can just select **Continue Setting up iPhone** for you to continue the setup and login into Apple ID. The transfer time depends on how much data that you are transferring. If you are transferring loads of videos and media, then it might take a little longer than if you are transferring tiny files.

III

Tips and tricks for the iPhone XS

Setting up Face ID

Well just like the iPhone X, you don't find the home button on the iPhone XS too. That's how it is now with the new iPhones. That's takes care of the Touch ID option. But it was a great way to unlock your phone and go through authentication process.

So Apple replaced it with Face ID. This one is much cooler and it's really not hard for you to set up Face ID

1. Open the **Settings** on the device. the icon with the gear symbol
2. Scroll down and select the option for **Face ID and Passcode.**
3. Now you want to enter in your passcode when you are asked to input it. You will need to enter in your 4 – 6 digits to continue with setting up Face ID. If you don't have a passcode for your device before, you can just skip

4. Now if you have not setup a passcode before, you want to select the option that says **Turn On Passcode**. Then you enter in a 6 digit passcode. If you want to set a passcode of a different length, you can just select **Passcode Options**
5. Select the option for **Set Up Face ID**
6. When you are prompted, select the option for **Get Started**.
7. Now a circle for you to scan should show up. Keep your eyes focused on the camera as you rotate your face. You may need to rotate your face more than once to complete the scan.
8. Hit **Continue**
9. You will be asked to rescan your face again. Just go through with the same process.
10. Select **Done**

Taking a screenshot

Well previously, one would have to press the home button along with the power to take a screenshot. But now with the home button gone, how can one take a screenshot. And you can't do without screenshots in this day and age.

But don't be confused, you can still take screenshots in your iPhone XS, you just have to press the **Power Button** and the **Volume Up Buttons** together at the same time. You'll see a small image of the screenshot you took to signify that it has been captured. The image will then be saved in the **Photos App**. But you can tap it to edit it just before it disappears.

Using Apple Pay

So you left your wallet at home, so what do you do? Take a 3 hour drive back home? No? Why stress when you have Apple Pay on your iPhone XS. With Apple Pay, you can pay for items with your smartphone in hand.

If you want to use Apple Pay, you just have to add your card to the wallet.
1. Enter the **Settings**
2. Go to **Wallet & Apple Pay**
3. Select **Add Card**
4. Before you can make use of the it, you may have to contact your bank to verify the card

When you have Apple Pay set up, you just have to tap the lock button twice (lock button at the right side of phone). If you have set up Face ID, your face will be scanned to proceed with the purchase.

Turning off your device

With previous iPhones, the button that you find at the side of the device is the power button. And you know that to lock the device, you would need to use the home button.

But now the button at the side is now the lock button. So how do your turn off your device? You just have to press and hold a **Volume Button** with the **Lock Button** at the same time. You will then see the option to slide and put off your iPhone.

Making use of portrait mode

On the iPhone XS, you have the portrait mode. You can make use of this feature both on the rear and the front cameras. If you would like to make use of portrait mode, all you just have to do is to open up the camera and then slide left on the menu slider that's along the bottom of the screen.

When you slide, you might be taken to another photo mode, you just have to keep sliding till you get to portrait mode. When you are in portrait mode, you can just take a photo like that or you can select from the list of light option.
- Natural light
- Stage light
- Contour light
- Studio light
- Stage light mono

You can choose the option that you would like to use to get your desired result. When you are in the light option, you just have to press the shutter button the normal way to take the shot. If you would rather use the front facing camera instead, you can simply just tap the rotate camera icon that's just next to the shutter button. The camera should switch now and you'll be able to take a photo with the front camera.

Creating a Memoji

The Animoji was released last year in the iPhone X for the iOS 11. But now, in the iOS 12 of the iPhone XS, there's the Memoji also. This are animated avatars that you can control when you alter your expression on your face.

It is very easy to create a Memoji on the iPhone XS,
- Enter the **Message** app
- Select the app drawer
- Choose the **Animoji** or **monkey** symbol
- Slide right till you the icon for a **New Memoji**
- From here, you'll be able to edit the Memoji to how you want to it to be.

When you are done with creating the Memoji, you can simply just hit the button for **Done**. You'll find this at the upper part of the screen. Your Memoji will now be saved.

Complete tasks with simple gestures

For a lot a people, the iPhone XS could very well be their first iPhone that doesn't have a home button. Other iPhones except the iPhone X actually has a home button. As a result of this lack of the home button, it would seem that navigating around the device would be much harder.

Well when you get the hang of things, you'll find that it's pretty easy to use. One gesture that you can use is the **swiping up from the bottom of the screen**. This action, will get you to easily switch between the apps that are open. When you do the swiping up, you'll also be able to quit the apps that you don't want to use by just sliding up from that app.

Another gesture that will be useful is the **swiping down from the top of the screen**.

When you swipe down from the middle of the screen, the notifications window will opened to you. If you swipe down from the right area, you'll see the control panel.

Apart from these, you can also use 2 quick gestures to be able to wake the phone up. The first one will have you **tap on the screen.** When you do this, it will wake the phone up. This gesture is available by default so you don't need to bother doing any searching in the settings. But if something got hold of your phone and it just suddenly switched it off, then you might want to turn it yourself

- Enter the **Settings**
- Choose **General**
- Then **Accessibility**
- Turn on the option to **Tap To Wake**.

For the other quick gestures, you will just have to **lift your phone up to wake** it. Just

like the previous setting, this one too is on by default on the iPhone XS. But just in case you want to disable it or you accidentally did so, you can see the option in
- **Settings**
- Select **Display and Brightness**
- Touch the slider for **Tap to Wake**

Using Do Not Disturb

Would you like to have a quiet time? That quiet time when no calls will enter to disturb peace. Or some less than important notification waking you up from your nap? Well your go to option should be Do Not Disturb.

Of course you can and would have solved the problem by simply switching your phone off. That's what many do. Some even go as far as taking out the battery to silence incoming calls and messages. But why go through that. We are in the new era, Do Not Disturb is the talk of the town.

You can enable it directly or you could do some editing to suit your preferences. To do this, you can just
   - Enter the **Settings**
   - Select **Do Not Disturb**

- You will now be able to make the needed changes that you want.

When you have set the features, you can just activate it by turning on the Do Not Disturb. Another option to activate is to select the Do Not Disturb icon in the control center (this is the icon that is depicted as a moon)

You can use the bedtime function to increase the usefulness of Do Not Disturb. This will get you to turn on some custom settings when it is bed time. This will dim the screen of the phone, dispatch the notification into the notification center and then of course silence calls. If you would like to set it up,
- Go to **Settings**
- Select **Do Not Disturb**
- Choose **Scheduled**
- Then **Bedtime**

Using split view on your iPhone XS

With the extra screen space and slim bezels of the iPhone XS, what good is it if you can't actually make use of all it? The split view option in the iPhone XS makes you do just that. You'll be able to get an expanded display for some websites and some apps.

What we are saying is that if you are in the Mail app for example and you are using split view, you'll be able to see your current messages and still see a preview screen. Split view also works for some other apps. It works for some websites like the New York Times

You don't have to go through too much stress if you want to make use of split view
- Open a website or an app that is compatible with split screen
- Switch your phone to landscape mode

- Make sure than the rotation lock is switched off. If you notice that the phone does not switch to landscape mode, then you can just slide downwards from the upper right and turn rotation lock off.

Using Siri

The famous Apple assistant; Siri is known for its ability to help you handle both simple and professional tasks. These tasks include setting some appointments in your calendar when you tell it to, using Apple pay to send money or to send messages.

Siri can also learn what your favourite choices are so that it will be able to give some shortcuts and suggestions that will be both useful and of interest to you.

You can make use of Siri with 2 easy ways
1. Press the lock button and hold
2. Just say 'Hey Siri'

But the second option to say hey Siri won't work unless you have actually set it up. To set up 'Hey Siri'
- Enter the **Settings**
- Choose **Siri & Search**

- Select **Listen For 'Hey Siri'**

Notifications

There have been some major changes to the notification in iOS 12. For example, you can now delete grouped messages in bulk when you just tap the **x** icon. If you would like to get the most out of the notification center, the best option is to customize it yourself to how you would prefer it.

Not only can you group notifications and delete them, you can also customize the notifications that you get in the notifications center. To do this, you just have to press and hold a notification and you'll see 2 selections to choose from. These are **Turn Off** and **Deliver Quietly**.

When you choose Deliver Quietly, this means that the notification will not alert you when it is received, it will just go to your notification center immediately.

With Turn Off, it just means that the particular app that you just long pressed will no longer send you notifications. But these are not the only customization that you can make for notifications. You can also go to

- **Settings**
- Then **Notifications**
- Select each of the app that you want to edit the notification settings of.

Set downtime

In the iPhone XS there the new feature that allow you to view how much you spend with your smartphone. When using our phones, the screen is mostly turned on. We can use the Screen Time in the settings to know how much the screen is being used

1. Go to **Settings**
2. Select **Screen Time**
3. Choose **Downtime** and turn on the option.
4. Set a time that you want to some apps and calls to be available

Control center

The control center on the iPhone XS can give you the opportunity to access the features that you use. You can get to it easily when you swipe down from the upper right of the display.

A lot of the icons that you find will be able to use 3D Touch so that you can see extra options. You just have to press hard on the particular icon that you want to view and then you'll see options come up for the app.

The control center is one of the most used features on the phone and it is very accessible. Just a swipe and you can get to features that you normally take forever to find. As a result of this, it would be totally cool if you were able to add some features that you make use of regularly. And guess what? You can.

All you have to do to customize the control center and edit the icon is
1. Move to the **Settings**
2. Select **Control Center**
3. Choose **Customize Controls**.
4. You can now include some controls that you want to be in the control center.

Using group FaceTime

With your iPhone XS, you can create a group FaceTime where you'll be able to include up to 32 people. This feature is available in iOS 12 and you can set up the group call when you go through the FaceTime app.

1. Open up the **FaceTime** app
2. Add the contacts that you would like to be part of the session.

In a group FaceTime call, you can add stickers, Animoji and texts to depict what you want. You can also participate in a group FaceTime when you are in an iMessage group chat.

1. When you are in the chat window, touch the initials that is at the top of the page
2. Touch the camera icon again

Keyboard in one handed mode

The iPhone XS is no small phone so using them with just one hand can prove to be a hassle. For it to be easier on you, Apple provided the one-handed keyboard. What this means is that the keyboard will be side lined to either the right or the left. It depends on the position that you selected. With the keyboard arranged to the side, it will be a lot easier to handle.

To this, you just have to
1. Slide into the **Settings**
2. Select **General**
3. Hit **Keyboards**
4. Choose **One Handed Keyboard**
5. Now you can now set where you want to the keyboard to display, right or left. Choose your preferred option

If you don't prefer to use this settings all the time, then that route is not the way to go. It's not every time that one will want to use the keyboard with one hand. So you can just turn it on and off as you wish through iMessage.

1. When the keyboard is opened, press and hold the icon that looks like a globe. (at the bottom left corner)
2. Select the side you want the keyboard to be, left or right.

If you are ready to make use of the keyboard with 2 hands and you want to turn it off, you just have to go through the same process.

1. Press the globe symbol in the keyboard
2. Select the option for the middle keyboard instead.

3.

IV

Tips and tricks for the iPhone XS Max

The home and unlock gestures

New users of the iPhone XS Max may find it hard to navigate the phone with the new 'no home button' rule. But when you spend some time to try to know how gestures are used in the device, you'll soon become a pro at it

If you want to unlock the phone, you just have to do the easy Tap to Wake gesture. When you tap the screen, you'll then be asked to Swipe to Unlock the iPhone. Another issue is the way to get to the home screen without the home button.

When the home button was still with us, just a press and we were at the home screen. But you can still easily get to home screen. You just have to swipe from the bottom of the screen from any app and you're in the home screen.

Taking a screenshot

No matter how much you run from it, you will need to take screenshots on your iPhone XS Max at some point. If you were using the older iPhones of course, you can just easily press the home button along with the power button to quickly take the shot. But now the process is a little different.

If you want to take a screenshot on your iPhone XS Max
- You want to navigate to the screen that you wish to take a screenshot of
- Then, press the sleep/wake button (or the side button) with the volume up button simultaneously.
- You will see the screen of the device flash and your screenshot will be taken.

Launching recent apps

To view your recent apps, you would previously have to press the home button twice. You'll then see the apps that you've recently made use of. Now that it's gone, it's very easy to get confused of how to see recent apps. And when you don't quit apps that run in the background, they'll eat more space and battery.

Most of the home buttons controls have been replaced with gestures. So now an easy gesture can just get the screen to open. But this is a bit more technical. From the bottom of the screen slide upwards, but not all the way up. Just till the middle of the screen and hold.

When you hold your finger in the middle for about a 1 second, you'll see the screen show up with the option to quit the apps

Hide your photos

I'm sure that no one loves the idea of someone creeping into their files and gallery to have a look at photos that they kept as confidential. Unfortunately just hiding the photo in a folder and naming it as PRIVATE won't get others to keep away. You've got to do more

And it's very easy to hide your photos in the iPhone XS Max.
- Fire up the **Photos** app
- Select the image that you wish to hide
- Hit the icon for **Share** (it's at the bottom left)
- Slide along and look for the option to **Hide**
- Touch **Hide Photo** for you to confirm that the image will be in a Hidden folder separate for the album folder.

With this, your photo is safe, and it won't get uploaded into the iCloud, moments or collections

Creating your Memoji

One great thing about the iPhone XS Max is that fact that it is armed with TrueDepth camera. It's a good thing that the iPhone XS Max has it because it allows you to be able to create your own Memoji. This is just like Animoji that's customized to resemble you. You can then use it in apps like iMessage.

You can choose from different hairstyles, accessories, eye colors and others. Just like Animoji, the Memoji follows the movement of your muscle. When you tap the record button, you'll be able to create a 30 second video that you can then send to your conversations on iMessage.

When the video is delivered, the recipient can then replay it when they tap the message. You can still play it if you'll like to see how it turned out.

Screen Time

Too addicted to the iPhone XS Max? Well it's understandable. The phone is really something, its tremendous features can make it hard to let of easily. As a result, there's a feature called Screen Time. This will get you to set limits for some apps.

You can also check how much you use your phone and then set some Downtime according to your preferences. With the Downtime option, you'll be able to set a time where your device will stop said apps from sending your notifications.

Saving your passwords

There's this feature the iOS 12 that is available on iPhone XS Max. It is called the Auto fill passwords. This will help you keep track of your passwords. The details that you input are then stored in the iCloud keychain.

You can also add your username and passwords for some certain sites and applications when you
1. Go to **Settings**
2. Then **Passwords & Accounts**
3. Choose **Website & App Passwords**
4. Then hit the **+** plus icon.

If you want to, you can select to verify with Face ID. It will now enter in your information when it notices one that has logged in already

Settings App Limits

One of the option of the Screen Time feature is the App Limits. This App Limit option will help you to reduce the amount of time that you use on some certain applications and games. The apps are sectioned according to their different categories.

So let's say that you choose to place some limit on the Social Networking. That just means that Facebook, Twitter, Snapchat will be restricted as their in that category. You can still set the days that you want to this limits that you set to last. If you would like it to last for a few minutes or some hours.

If would like to set App Limits
- Enter the **Settings**
- Select **Screen Time**
- Then **App Limits**

- Select the categories that you like to place some limits on
- Touch **Add**.
- When you have set the time limits for the category, you can then hit **App Limits** to set the limits automatically.

If you have set a limit for an app and you tap it, you'll be shown an hourglass symbol. When you open the app, you'll be given a notification to tell you that you have gotten to the limit. If you still wish to use the app maybe for an urgent reason, you can just ignore the limit through the whole day. You can also choose to use the app for about 15 minutes then you'll get a reminder about the placed App Limit.

Measuring objects with your mobile

With the help of Apples ARKit, users of the iPhone XS Max are able to measure real life spaces and objects with the camera on their smartphone. When you use Measure, you'll be able to get the measurements of things like posters, frames, sings or pictures.

1. Open up the app
2. Set your camera to point at the object in question
3. Go through with the options given on how you get the things well aligned.
4. Touch the display so that you can see the measurements

Any conversions that you make will be shown in centimetres and inches. Though it's true that this will not give you an accurate and precise measurement, it's quite useful to have around.

Depth control

One cool feature that iPhone users are loving is the depth control feature. This does exactly what it say; controls the depth of field.

In other words, it will help you to control the amount of blur that is made to background of an image. Now the cool part it that, you can actually do this after the picture has been taken.

If you want to use depth control, you just have to

1. Select the photo that you want to change
2. Choose **Edit**
3. Use the depth control slider to edit.

Force close apps on the iPhone XS Max

Previously on older iPhones, you would need to get to the apps switcher then swipe from the bottom corner of the screen for you to close an app. You will then press and hold the app in question till you see the red minus sign that is shown at the top left.

But with the iPhone XS Max, the method is quite different and it's a lot simpler. You don't need to press and hold anything. All you just have to do is to slide up from the bottom of the screen then swipe the apps that you want to close. Very easy.

Add stickers and edit photos with iMessage

When you make use of the camera app in iMessage, you will be able to do some editing when you hit the star symbol that's at the bottom left corner of the screen. You will then switch to the selfie camera.

With this you now be able to include accessories like stickers which you may download from the app store if you would like. You can also include Memoji, Animoji or shapes. When you are through with adding your decorations, you can then hit the X for you to hit the camera shutter

If agree with the photo that was taken, you can then hit the blue arrow to set it in the message window.

View the battery performance

If you want to check how your battery is faring, you can just
- Slide in the **Settings**
- Choose **Battery**

Now you'll see graphs to show you the level of your battery and the way you used it in the last 24 hours. You'll also a detailed report that shows you the amount of time that you spend with the screen on and the screen off. You'll find this below.

You'll also see the percentage of the battery power that the apps are using. You can't only view these details over the course of 24 hours, you can switch to view the usage of over 10 days. Switch according you to your preference

This feature was first launched with the iOS 11 and it will allow to see the Battery

Health Information when you select the option for Battery Health in the graph. But now in the iOS 12 in iPhone XS Max, you also get insights and suggestions option for the Battery Health feature. This will give you the various ways that your battery life can be improved

How to manage group notifications

Notification that are in the lock screen are grouped in the iPhone XS Max. When you swipe left on a particular notification, you can then select the option for **Manage**. This will then give you 2 options **Turn Off** and **Deliver Quietly**.

When you choose Deliver Quietly, it just means that the notification that you receive will not show up in the lock screen but just quietly pass onto the notification center. When you choose Turn Off, the notification will not only stop showing in the lock screen but be restricted completely.

When you select **Settings**, you will be able to select if you would prefer the notification grouped. When you choose **Automatic**, the notification will be grouped in separate stacks though by the same apps. What this means is that, if you get a text message from 2 different individuals, the message will be stacked in 2 different sections.

You can also select the option to group **By app**. This will compile all the text messages so that it will be in one stack. It doesn't matter if its different texts, it's will be compiled. If you would like to just go back to the default way of the notifications showing up in the lock screen, you can just turn off the option in settings

Enable Do Not Disturb for bedtime

In the iPhone XS Max, the whole settings for the Do Not Disturb feature got a remix. This change now allows users to be able to edit the settings to their preferences. You now have extra editing options. Not only can you just set the feature to work on certain times of the day, you can also get to Do Not Disturb in the settings then switch on the **Bedtime** option.

This can silence all the notifications that you get till the morning. But it all depends on how long you set it. The screen of the device will be dimmed and then show only the date and time. When this happens, then you know that your phone has switched to that mode.

V

Troubleshooting the iPhone XS and iPhone XS Max

The iPhone XS and the iPhone XS Max are the best when it comes to the latest iPhone line-up. It is packed with many cool features. Like for example the OLED display is top notch, you can also opt for the higher storage option. And this can get as high as 512 GB.

The camera too is just marvellous and some say that is might just be the best out there. The A12 bionic processor will get you to enjoy your phone without any sluggishness or hangs. But the fact that it has all these wonderful features, does not mean that it is without its flaws. It is made by humans so you shouldn't expect utter perfection.

The iPhone XS and iPhone XS Max comes it its own troubles and it has been noticed by many users. There have been reports when using the devices. If you too are facing some issues with your phone, then this is for you. We are going to discuss about the different iPhone problems and how to fix it. Even if you have not faced these before, it is best to pay attention so you'll know what to do if something like these happen.

iPhone refuses to charge

It's very common to hear people report that their iPhone XS does not charge when they try to charge it. They connect the charger to the outlet and plug it in their device but still doesn't charge. The solution is not far-fetched. In some devices, the charging will not start when it is in sleep mode. This should not be the case but when many tap the phone it starts to charge

1. You want to first check the iOS version of your device. You want make sure that it is using the latest software that was released for iOS devices. iOS 12.0

2. Whenever you encounter some problem as you try to charge the device, you can just
   - Enter **Settings**
   - Then go to **General**
   - Select **Software Update**.

This will get ensure that you have the latest version of the software for your device. When you get the software updated, you should have to problem with charging the device. Try charging and see what happens.

Face ID problems

Apart from the iPhone X, the iPhone XS and XS Max are the only iPhones that allow you to make use of Face ID to unlock your phone or for other authentication. The other iPhones make use of Touch ID. But many encounter issues with the Face ID process as the try to set it up. To help to solve the problem, follow through with these solutions

1. When you try to register your face and Face ID fails, you have to make sure that you are in a well-lit environment. If you are in a room, make sure you're near the window or another source of light.

2. Users of the device also find it hard to use the feature when they have set it up already. If you face problems as you try to unlock your device with Face ID, you have to place the phone

in a position where it can see your face well. Then stare at the screen actively

3. The Face ID feature will register your face when you set it up. So if you change your appearance, it won't register it

4. If you still find issues with the feature after doing this, you can try to contact Apple support. You can also try a service center, but make sure that they are authorized

Wi-Fi is too slow

When they try to use a Wi-Fi network or data, some have noticed that it just becomes too slow.

1. You can try to
- Enter the **Settings**
- Select **General**
- Choose **Reset**
- Then choose the option that says **Reset Network Settings.**
   Now you will have to enter in the Wi-Fi password again. This can help to raise the speed back to normal
2. Another thing that can cause this is the software. And of course when you have software issues, you'll have to go check if you are using the latest version of the software for the device. If you are not, then you want to enter the settings, and get the software upgraded

Problems with Bluetooth connecting

The iPhone XS has Bluetooth 5.0 when it was released. And this has been around on the device for some time now so that the technological improvements can be strengthened. With such kind of Bluetooth, what you should expect is nothing short of super speed when using the Bluetooth feature. Also when transferring data, the range should also be better.

But while you get that, the feature too is not without blemish. Some have reported that the have encountered some problems as they try to connect with a different device using Bluetooth. If you ever face this problem, here are the things you should do

1. When you are in the home screen
- Enter the **Settings**

- Then select **Bluetooth** for it to get it switched off
- When you are sure that it is turned off, wait for a couple of seconds then turn it back on.
  Now try to connect and see what happens
2. If that didn't work, then I've got one more thing up my sleeve. It is software update. Yes without an update in the device software, things will not function normally. So check if you have the latest software for your device and then
- Go to **Settings**
- Then select **General**
- Choose **Software Update**.
- Install the updates for your iPhone properly

Smoothing is too harsh

Though this problem is not as 'life-threatening' as the others, but it is still an issue. This happens when you smoothen the subject as you try to take a picture. As you do this, you may notice that the effect becomes harsh. This might because of the way that the new camera of the iPhone XS works. And it doesn't seem like a real solution will come soon as Apple wants to be harsher

1. One thing that you can definitely do is to turn off Smart HDR. When you do this, there's a chance that the harsh effect of the camera will be reduced. If you are using the front camera, you might not notice the difference
2. The next thing to do is to find out other apps that are perfect for taking

pictures. When you change the camera, you might find better results.

Battery constantly reduces

Yes, Apple has done a great job when it comes to the battery life of their phones. The iPhone XS and iPhone XS Max have great battery life compared to their previous phones. But still the battery life may not be enough. In the iOS 12, you'll find a feature titled; Battery Health. This will help to show you how the battery is used in your phone. You'll see which apps take more power.

There've been many users complaining about how the batter of their iPhone XS devices constantly drains. To solve this, you want to find out reason why this is happen and then trying a fix

1. The first thing that should come to your mind when you notice this problem is that there is an app that is

sucking the life of the battery. So stop this

- Move to the **Settings**
- Select **Battery** so that you'll see the apps that are consuming more power than the others
- Look for the app that is taking more power. When you find it, you want to take it out.

  This should get the phone working properly

2. So if that doesn't work than you want to try to switch background app refresh off. If you would like to turn it off
- Enter the **Settings**
- Choose **General**
- Then select **Background Refresh App**.

  Now notice if the trouble still persists
3. You can also try to back up your iPhone with iTunes or iCloud to help fix the issue of battery drainage

Problems with iCloud restoring on the device

Speaking of iCloud, some have encountered problem in that regard. They try to update the settings of the iCloud then the iPhone device just hangs when it is halfway through. If this ever happens, your best option is to do a hard reset

1. You want to make the iPhone XS device to do a restart. To do this, you want to
- Press the volume up button then release.
- Press the volume down button then release.
- Hold down the side button till you see the Apple logo light up. Now the iPhone device should reboot without wasting time.
When the power of the phone comes back on. You can then retry the

iCloud updating process again and see if it works this time.

2. You should also try to restore the process by creating something like a backup on your computer then redo the updating action.

3. If you cannot still figure out the problem, you can go through the guide Apple created.

Wi-Fi connection issues

Some users have complained that the iPhone XS takes time before is actually connects to a Wi-Fi network. In fact, sometimes it might not even connect at all. Wi-Fi network issues usually happen when there a software update released by Apple. When you do a hard reset, you can also solve this issue of Wi-Fi not connecting.

1. So you want to perform a hard reset. To do this, you will need to
- Press the volume up button then release.
- Then very quickly, press the volume down button and release.
- Follow up with pressing and holding the side button on the device will the Apple logo shows up.
- Try to reconnect and see if that worked

2. If the hard reset solution didn't work, then you will have to try resetting the settings of the network. To this
- Slide into the **Settings**
- Then hit **General**
- Select **Reset**
- Choose the option that reads **Reset Network Settings**. You will now need to wait for a few minutes for the process to be completed.

   This method will clear the current network settings on the device and revert it to the default. You will need to input the Wi-Fi password again

3. You can also try restarting the router. When the router is back on, try connecting the iPhone XS back to the network and see what happens

Problem with the sound

When you try to play audio with the speakers of your iPhone XS or iPhone XS Max, you should get a clear, and loud sound. But sometimes, what you'll get will be muffled and even cracked at times. It can be very frustrating when this happens. But here are some things can you can try to solve the problem.

1. You should try doing a hard reset or just restart the iPhone. Press the volume up button then the volume down button. Press and hold the side button to perform a hard reset
2. If the issue still continues, you can switch on the Bluetooth then switch it off again.
3. Make sure that there's no debris obstructing the speaker or the lighting dock.

4. If you make use of a case for your iPhone, you want to remove it then try enabling LTE
5. Try restoring the device from backup and if that doesn't work, contact Apple and tell them about the problem that you are experiencing.

Issues with cellular data

Speaking of LTE, users of the iPhone XS also face problem when they try to use the cellular data on the device. There be no service at all. While you can try to restart your phone, you may also want to contact your service provider to help you figure out what the problem is

1. Do a hard reset or restart the device
2. Toggle off and on the cellular data.
- Enter the **Settings**
- Select **Cellular Data**
- Choose **Cellular Data Options**
- Then enable **LTE**
- Turn data off

DISCLAIMER

In as much as the author believes beginners will find this book helpful in learning how to operate both the iPhone XS and XS Max, it is only a small book. It should not be relied upon solely for all iPhone XS and XS Max tricks and troubleshooting.

ABOUT THE AUTHOR

Stephen Stone has been a certified apps developer and tech researcher for more than 12 years. Some of his 'how to' guides have appeared in a handful of international journals and tech blogs.